HORSEMANSHIP
Basics for More Advanced Riders

Also by Evelyn Pervier

Horsemanship: Basics for Beginners
Horsemanship: Basics for Intermediate Riders

HORSEMANSHIP
Basics for More Advanced Riders

Written and Illustrated by
Evelyn Pervier

Photographs by

Melinda Hughes

JULIAN MESSNER   New York

Copyright © 1984 by Evelyn Pervier

Published by Julian Messner, a division of
Simon & Schuster, Inc.
Simon & Schuster Building,
1230 Avenue of the Americas,
New York, New York 10020.

JULIAN MESSNER and colophon are trademarks of
Simon & Schuster, Inc.

Manufactured in the United States of America

Design by Irving Perkins Associates

Library of Congress Cataloging in Publication Data.
Pervier, Evelyn.
  Horsemanship, basics for more advanced riders.

  Bibliography: p.
  Includes index.
  Summary: Suggestions for showing horses, for leasing
or sponsoring them, for breeding and raising them, and
for administering first aid and emergency care.
  1. Horsemanship—Juvenile literature. [1. Horseman-
ship] I. Hughes, Melinda, ill. II. Title.
SF309.2.P475 1983   798.2   83-42783
ISBN 0-671-45521-4

For Melanie, with love

ACKNOWLEDGMENTS

I would like to thank all my friends who loaned me their bodies, their horses, and their advice for this book, especially:

Raymond Deiter, V.M.D.	Sally Mays
Anne Felix	Lisa Miller
Samantha Hecht	Jenifer Morris
Nancy Horowitz	Andy Nichols
Melinda Hughes	Michael Reibin
Paul Hughes	Barbara Rohan
Larry Larson	Kathy Rohan
Scott Loring	Bitsy Shields
Ruth Maher	Audrey Stroup

CONTENTS

HORSEMANSHIP
Basics for More Advanced Riders

CHAPTER 1

THE HORSE IN MOTION

IMAGINE A BALLERINA dancing in *Swan Lake* with a monkey clinging to her back, or a track star sprinting to the finish line with a puppy perched on his shoulders. The idea is, of course, ludicrous, but think about it. This is exactly what we expect the horse to do. Horses are the only animals expected to compete as athletes, to run in races, jump fences, and participate in marathons while carrying a creature of another species on their backs. This arrangement often presents certain difficulties for horses, especially young ones, which have enough problems just sorting out four legs and balancing themselves without the additional weight of a rider to contend with.

When horses are playing freely together, they cavort and frisk with a grace and elegance that never fails to move the horse-lover. It is this graceful freedom of movement that horsemen have always coveted—that the horse is able to achieve this beauty *despite* the rider sitting astride his back. To help you understand this unique and harmonious relationship between human and horse, you, as the rider, should have some knowledge of equine balance and movement, both on the flat and over fences.

If you look at a horse you will notice that the front legs have to support far more body weight than the rear legs. They carry the weight of the head, the neck, the chest, and part of the barrel, while the rear legs carry the other half of the barrel and

The horse in motion, an exciting combination of elegance and power.

the quarters. Yet, surprisingly, it is the back legs, carrying only 40 percent of the horse's total body weight, that actually propel the horse's body forward and his rear end that acts as the equine power pack.

Where does the rider sit in relation to this unequal distribution of horsepower? If you draw an imaginary line from behind the withers to the ground, this will approximate the horse's center of gravity. The rider sits astride the horse's back at this center of gravity, and from this position is able to influence the horse's movement. Despite the rider's weight, the object of good riding is to enable the horse's rear end (his engine) to function properly at each gait, with the hind legs reaching

Although the horse's front legs support more body weight, it is the powerful hind quarters and hind legs which actually propel the animal forward.

under the body, propelling the horse forward and into the bridle.

During the course of his training, the horse has to learn to accept the weight of the rider. But even more important, the horse has to learn how to balance his own body plus this additional burden. For young horses learning to accept this additional load, the muscles of the back and quarters have to be strengthened considerably before the former all-important balance can be regained. This takes hours of patient schooling, but once this strength has been achieved and the animal's natural balance reestablished, the result is a harmonious relationship between horse and rider.

It is even more difficult for the horse to balance himself while carrying a rider over a fence than it is on the flat. Here balance of both horse and rider becomes even more critical. As the horse approaches a jump he stretches and lowers his neck, readying himself. As he takes off, he raises his head and shortens his neck, at the same time lifting and folding his two front legs. At this point, the horse can't see the jump at all; all the visual calculations concerning the jump's height and width have to be made during his approach. Next he springs up and

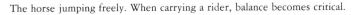

The horse jumping freely. When carrying a rider, balance becomes critical.

forward, stretching his head and neck out ahead of his body. The hind legs follow the bascule (the arc) as he suspends over the jump. Completing the arc, the horse lands on one foot (1,000 pounds of horseflesh lands on one tiny foot every time the horse jumps). When he lands, the head comes up again, shortening the neck, and the other front leg comes forward to take over just before the hind legs reach the ground.

As you can imagine, it takes an honest horse to carry an inexperienced rider over a fence. The beginning rider tends to lurch about, inadvertently banging the horse on the back and in the mouth, playing havoc with the horse's own sense of balance. This is why the combination of green horse/green rider is so disastrous. With both participants struggling to maintain their balance and with neither really kowing what he is doing, the result is often a loss of confidence for both partners.

Once you start to understand how your weight influences the horse when you ride in relation to the animal's own problems with balance and movement, then you are on your way to becoming a serious rider.

CHAPTER 2

THE SERIOUS RIDER

THE SERIOUS RIDER is far more than a superior riding technician; she is subtle, intuitive, sympathetic, and, above all, patient. With these virtues she is able to understand the capabilities, sensitivity, and the tolerance level of each horse as an individual and to ride that horse accordingly. It takes time to arrive at this point, but this is one of the satisfying rewards of riding; knowing that the art of horsemanship is a lifetime commitment and that most training programs take time and cannot be rushed.

Personalities play an important role in equitation. Often not enough attention is devoted to matching horse and rider. For instance, the nervous, temperamental horse requires a firm, quiet rider who will give the animal confidence. The lazy, mellow animal needs a lively rider, one who will keep him alert and interested to prevent him from becoming bored during schooling.

Knowing when to reward and when to punish the horse is another vital aspect of horsemanship. Rewarding the horse consists of talking to him in a soothing voice, riding him on a loose rein after a particularly hard school, stroking his neck gently, or maybe giving him an apple or a carrot after a satisfying school. The horse quickly and intuitively starts to understand these rewards, and most will strive to please rather than disobey. After all, horses don't want trouble any more than riders do.

17

Punishing a horse should not conjure up visions of clubs and chains. Rather it consists of using your voice to scold, your hand to slap, your legs to drive. Sometimes it is simply the absence of reward. With a lazy horse you may need to implement these aids with spurs or a whip. Whenever punishment is appropriate, the most important point to remember is that it should be carried out *immediately* after a disobedience, or not at all. For instance, if your horse refuses a low schooling fence, don't wait five minutes to punish him. He won't understand why he is being punished. The horse isn't capable of making the connection between cause and effect unless the punishment is administered at the time of the disobedience.

When should the horse be punished? This is where the thinking horseman carefully assesses the situation before rushing in with a punishment. Generally speaking, it is usually the inexperienced rider, failing to understand *why* the horse is misbehaving, who resorts to punishment, making the situation worse in the process. For instance, maybe the horse is misbehaving because he is truly afraid of something. If this is the case, then he shouldn't be punished at all, but should be quietly and firmly encouraged to overcome the fear.

Sometimes horses misbehave because they are "high" as a result of too much rich food and too little exercise. It would be unkind to punish a horse for unruly high spirits since he is hardly to blame for his diet and lack of exercise. The rider should understand the cause of this playful foolishness, and either turn the horse out to play or longe him for a while until the horse is ready to settle down to work.

It takes some horses longer than others to understand and interpret the rider's wishes. A horse should never be punished simply because he doesn't understand what the rider wants him to do. It is up to the rider to know whether or not the horse has had sufficient training to understand the equitation cues and to give clear aids accordingly.

As the serious rider advances slowly up the equitation ladder, she becomes capable of attempting and performing certain movements designed to balance the horse and improve her own equitation skills. Before attempting any new exercise, your horse should be warmed up so that he is relaxed both physically and mentally. If your horse is nervous or tense, it is hard to get his cooperation to attempt a new movement.

You are now ready to put your horse *on the bit*. It is through this contact with the horse's mouth that the rider guides and regulates the horse's movement. You accomplish this by maintaining a soft, equal feel of the horse's mouth, asking him to lower his head and seek a mutual contact with you. Try to imagine that the reins are made of elastic. Squeeze them sensitively and alternately with each hand to encourage the horse to lower his head. At the same time use your seat and legs to bring the horse's body *into the bridle*. When you have successfully accomplished putting your horse on the bit, he will relax

Behind the bit. The horse is avoiding the contact of the rider's hands by bending his head in towards his chest.

his jaw and take a soft hold of the bit; his head will remain steady at each gait.

Sometimes a horse will get *behind the bit.* This means that he is avoiding the contact of the rider's hands by bending his head in toward his chest and dropping the bit. This often happens when a horse has been consistently ridden by a rider with bad hands. The horse finally learns how to protect himself by avoiding contact with the bit altogether.

The other extreme is the horse that gets *above the bit* by carrying his head high and hollowing his back. This horse also avoids contact with the bit by angling his head so high that the bit works off the corners of his lips rather than the bars of his mouth, where it should rest. Many green horses get above the bit because they are learning to balance their bodies with the additional weight of the rider. It takes time for the horse to learn to balance himself and lower his head to accept the bit willingly.

Now the horse is above the bit, avoiding contact with it by angling his head so high that the bit works off the corners of the lips rather than the bars of the mouth.

When a horse leans on the bit, he is said to be *over the bit*. Sometimes a horse will evade the bit by pushing his tongue over it. This annoying habit can be easily cured by the use of a drop-noseband, which keeps the mouth closed so that the horse doesn't have room to wriggle his tongue over the bit.

One of the best exercises to supple a horse is the *shoulder-in*. This exercise helps the horse to bend his spine and flex his hocks, but it only works to loosen up the horse if it is performed correctly. For many horses, bending the spine is uncomfortable, so they try to "fake" a shoulder-in by merely bending the neck rather than the spine. To perform a shoulder-in to the left, trot the horse as if about to start a bend. Hold your inside leg firmly on the girth, with your right leg behind the girth to control the horse's impulsion, to prevent

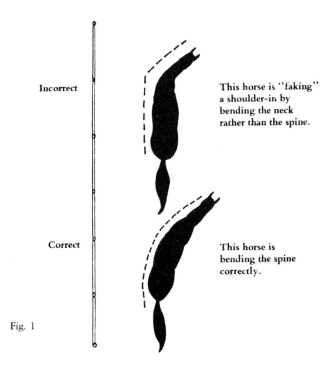

Incorrect

This horse is "faking" a shoulder-in by bending the neck rather than the spine.

Correct

This horse is bending the spine correctly.

Fig. 1

The turn on the forehand. The horse is being asked to move his quarters in even steps around the inner foreleg, while at the halt.

his hind legs from moving off the track. In other words, you want the horse to bend his body around your inside leg while moving forward. When performed correctly and viewed from head-on, the horse can be seen moving on three tracks: the outside rear leg on one track, the inside rear and outside front leg on the middle track, and the inside front leg on the inside track.

Another of the more advanced exercises is the *turn on the forehand*. This movement is performed from the halt. The horse is asked to move his quarters in even steps around the inner foreleg. To achieve a turn on the forehand with the quarters moving to the left, use your right leg behind the girth to push the horse around sideways away from your leg, while supporting the mouth with the right rein.

Many dressage and equitation tests demand that the rider *counter-canter* his horse. This means asking your horse to canter on the wrong lead intentionally. This difficult test demands a willing, obedient, and well-balanced horse that will pick up either lead when asked by the rider. The counter-canter may be performed in a circle, a serpentine, or, most difficult, a figure eight.

You may sometimes question the value of all these balancing and suppling exercises. After all, does it really matter whether or not your horse can turn on the forehand, perform a shoulder-in, or counter-canter? Is it really that important that he is on the bit, not behind, above, or over it? The answer is that it is much more pleasant to ride a relaxed, willing, and obedient horse than a stiff, unruly animal that resents being ridden. What these schooling exercises accomplish are camaraderie, obedience, and understanding with the added bonus that both horse and rider get physically fit.

CHAPTER 3

SCHOOLING FOR THE SHOW RING

SOONER OR LATER most riders decide that they would like to show their horses. It might be for the challenge of competition or simply for the fun of participating in the sport. Whatever your reasons are for deciding to show, a certain amount of mental and physical preparation is necessary for both you and your horse if you want to compete successfully. Competing successfully, however, does not necessarily mean winning silver plates and countless ribbons. The successful competitor competes for the personal satisfaction of performing well under pressure, whether or not that effort is rewarded with a prize.

The first step to successful showing is to plan it all out, allowing plenty of time to prepare yourself and your horse for the coming event. If you dash off on a whim to the first show that comes along, you are almost certainly doomed to disaster. Successful showing takes planning, preparation, and a lot of schooling.

Generally speaking, horse show managers send out the entry forms (premium lists) several weeks prior to an event. Be sure to pick a show that is well within your scope as a rider. If you choose a show designed for horses and riders more advanced than you are, you will probably find yourself

For your first show, choose a show that is well within your range as a rider.

hopelessly outclassed and end up feeling rather discouraged. Study the entry form carefully and consider your horse's physical condition and ability before deciding which events to enter. If your horse can comfortably jump three feet but balks at jumping anything higher, then enter him in classes that specify the fences will be no higher than three feet. You also must consider how many classes you should enter, and whether or not you can get your horse conditioned in time. It is hard on a horse to enter, for instance, three flat classes in a row, particularly if the weather is hot or humid. Try to arrange the classes so that the horse can rest in between events.

Once the classes have been chosen and the entry sent in, you can plan your course of action. Make sure you use your time wisely to prepare properly for the upcoming event.

Condition yourself for the show by working without stirrups to tighten your legs.

Physically Conditioning Your Horse   Showing is hard on a horse. When show day finally arrives, it is your responsibility as a horseman to be sure that your animal is as fit and ready—both physically and mentally—as you are. Remember, going to the show is your idea, not your horse's. Given the choice he would probably prefer to stay home and munch hay in the comfort of his stall or paddock. At the show he is going to be subjected to all the excitement of a strange place, with unusual smells and sights and other horses to distract him. He is going to feel nervous and tense at first, and exceedingly tired later. Your first responsibility then is to condition your horse so that he is fit and ready for the occasion.

Conditioning your horse means planning a regular routine of ring work, interspersed with plenty of trail riding so that the animal doesn't become bored and soured by working endless circles in the arena. Plan your routine so that you can work on something different each day. For instance:

Day One: Work in the ring, practicing your equitation at the walk, trot, and canter. Work without stirrups to tighten your legs.

Day Two: Trail ride, working on lengthening and shortening your horse's stride, transitions, and canter departs from the walk on each lead.

Day Three: Back to the ring to school over low fences.

Day Four: Fun trail ride, with no specific schooling. Just enjoy the ride and stay out for at least two hours.

Day Five: Short school on the flat in the ring, working on any problems you may have. Then surprise your horse by going for a quick outing on the trail.

Day Six: Another school over fences, this time at the height over which you will be showing. Don't overdo it.

Day Seven: Day off for both of you.

Mentally Conditioning Your Horse   You are probably wondering how you can mentally prepare your horse for the upcoming event. The answer is to prepare him sufficiently so that the show is not totally surprising and overwhelming. For instance,

Your horse's show conditioning program should include some fun trail rides with varied ring work.

if you are planning to jump a course of fences at the show, then you must practice jumping a course of fences several times during your schooling sessions. It would not be fair to expect your horse to face quarter-rounds, oxers, and gates, if he has never seen any of these fences before. If you know that the show is going to be held in an indoor arena, and your horse has never worked in one before, it would be a good idea to arrange to school in one prior to the show. Anything you can do to prepare your horse for the sights and situations he will have to face at the show is to your advantage as a competitor.

CHAPTER **4**

BRAIDING FOR THE SHOW RING

IF YOU ARE going to show your horse, then it is an excellent idea to learn how to braid his mane and tail. With practice, braiding is relatively easy. Knowing how to do it yourself can save you hundreds of dollars if you plan to show frequently. For any show other than a schooling show, it is mandatory that the mane be braided. Braiding is one of the few areas where the thrifty rider can economize.

Mane Braiding   It is much easier to accomplish a good braiding job if the mane has been thinned out and shortened to about four or five inches in length. If you want your braiding to look professional, then each braid should be exactly the

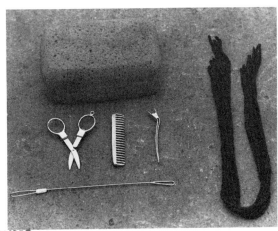

The mane braiding kit should include a sponge, yarn, a pull-through, a small mane comb, a large hair clip (or bobby pin), and a pair of scissors.

Divide out approximately two inches of mane with your comb, and fasten the remaining hair out of the way with the hair clip. Plait down the braid, and halfway down, thread in one of the pieces of yarn so that it becomes a part of the braid. Tie off the yarn at the end of the braid, but don't cut off the loose ends.

To turn up the braid, thread the ends of the yarn through the eye of the pull-through. Bend the braid under by inserting the pull-through needle through the base of the mane from underneath.

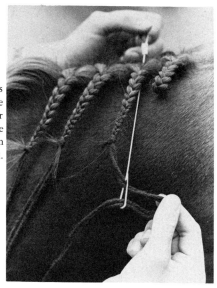

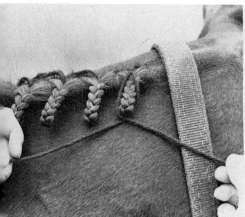

Crisscross the yarn behind the braid.

Tie off the braid firmly in the middle . . .

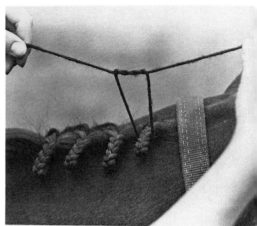

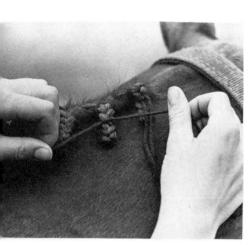

. . . using a double knot.

Snip off the ends of the yarn neatly.

same size and shape. These are the supplies you will need in order to braid:

Damp sponge
Yarn cut into twelve-inch lengths (about twenty-four pieces)
Pull-through or a large-eyed darning needle (pull-throughs can be purchased from most tack stores)
Small mane comb
Large bobby pin
Pair of scissors

Stand on a stool and dampen the mane with your sponge. Then, starting behind the ears, divide approximately two inches of mane with your mane comb. Using the large bobby pin, fasten the remainder of the mane hair out of your way while you plait this braid. Try to braid the hair uniformly. When you are halfway down, thread in one of the pieces of yarn so that it becomes a part of the braid. When you reach the end of the hair, tie the yarn in a knot around the base of the braid. Don't cut off the remaining yarn since you will need this later. Continue down the entire mane in this manner, making sure that each braid is tightly plaited and the same size. To turn up the braid, thread the ends of the yarn hanging from the finished braid through the eye of the pull-through. Bend the braid under, inserting the pull-through needle through the base of the mane from underneath. Pull the yarn through, remove the pull-through, and crisscross the yarn behind the braid, finishing on top. Tie the braid with a double knot and cut off the excess yarn.

The first time you attempt to braid, it may take an hour of utter frustration to complete the job. Your horse will fidget and shake his head at the most inappropriate moment, and you will convince yourself that it is the worst braiding job ever attempted. Take heart. With practice you will undoubtedly

The finished braid job.

become an excellent braider, able to finish a mane in thirty minutes or less.

Tail Braiding   Once you can braid the mane, tail braiding will be a cinch. And tails are far more interesting to braid than manes. Unlike the mane, it is not mandatory to braid the tail for show purposes. For a variety of reasons, however, it is often advisable to do so. For instance, if your horse has a short, skimpy tail you may want to tidy up his appearance by hiding the unattractive tail with a braided mud knot. On the other hand, if your horse has a gloriously long tail, it is possible to enhance his elegant appearance still further by French-braiding the tail. Whatever the style, you must start out with a clean and untangled tail.

French Braid   Once you have the knack, a French braid should take around fifteen minutes to do. The most difficult

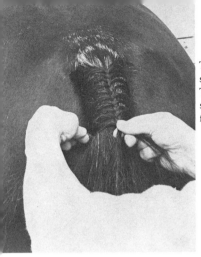

To start a French braid, take a few hairs from each side of the tail and cross them over each other firmly. Then take a few hairs from the center of the tail and start braiding down the center, taking a few hairs from each side.

part of this braid is the top of the tail where the braid starts, since the hairs are short and slip through your fingers. It helps to dampen these hairs with a sponge. To start the braid, take a few hairs from each side of the tail and cross these over each other firmly. Then take a few hairs from the center of the tail so that you now have three separate strands of hair. Start braiding down the center of the tail, taking a few hairs from either side and keeping the braid straight, firm, and quite tight. When you arrive at a point about two inches above the end of the tailbone, take no more hair from each side of the tail, but continue to plait the center braid for a few more inches. Braid in a piece of yarn, just as you did with the mane, to finish off the braid. There are several ways to put the finishing touches

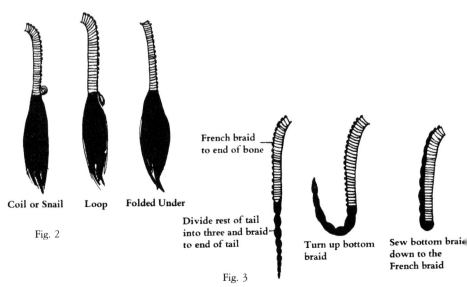

Coil or Snail   Loop   Folded Under

Fig. 2

French braid to end of bone

Divide rest of tail into three and braid to end of tail

Turn up bottom braid

Sew bottom braid down to the French braid

Fig. 3

French braid to base of tail-bone. Divide remaining hair into three equal parts.

Braid down two or three times. Divide remaining hair into two equal parts.

Fold back and crisscross hair in front and behind tail, working upwards. Finish braid by taking small piece of hair from under the French braid, plait this with your two loose ends, secure with yarn, and tuck into the folds of the knot. For additional security, sew.

Fig. 4

1. Divide hair into three.

2. Braid twice; divide remaining hair into two equal parts.

3. Fold back and crisscross hair in front and behind tail, working up.

4. Take the two tail ends a. and b.

5. Make a small braid using a small piece of loose hair from the center front (c.). Secure braid and tuck into folds of knot.

Fig. 5

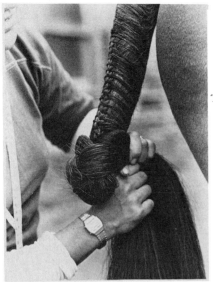

Tying up a braided mud knot.

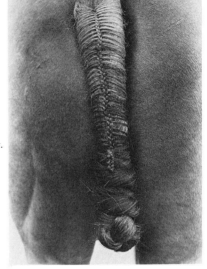

The finished braided mud knot.

on your French braid. You can fold the end of the braid under and sew it; you can make a neat loop of braided hair; or you can roll the braid firmly into a coil, sewing it securely into place.

Once you know how to accomplish the French braid, it is quite easy to master two other variations of tail braiding: the braided mud tail (See Fig. 3) and the braided mud knot (See Fig. 4).

If you don't care to braid your horse's tail at all, but would simply like to tie it up in some way to protect it from mud and brambles, then you need to know how to tie a simple mud knot (See Fig. 5).

CHAPTER 5

SHOW TURN OUT

ALL SUCCESSFUL SHOW riders seem to have one characteristic in common, whether they are showing on the flat or over fences. They have "presence" in the ring; a subtle, intangible mixture of calm confidence combined with an immaculate appearance. This special look doesn't happen by accident. It is the result of hours of preparation and an almost fanatical attention to detail.

What to Wear   Riding clothes are protective, traditional, and very elegant. They are designed to be comfortably functional and, at the same time, provide you with maximum protection against chafing and rubbing while riding and against injuries to your head should you be unfortunate enough to fall. When purchasing riding clothes for the show ring, choose conservative, dark colors for your velvet hunt cap and riding jacket, and either brick, beige, tan, or gray for your breeches or jodhpurs. If you want to personalize your appearance somewhat, girls may have their chokers monogrammed or wear a small pin and boys may wear a conservative tie. Flashy colors and flamboyant styles have no place in the show ring. Quiet elegance should be your keynote.

Hunt Cap   Velvet or velveteen, either black or navy. Some hard hats come equipped with a detachable har-

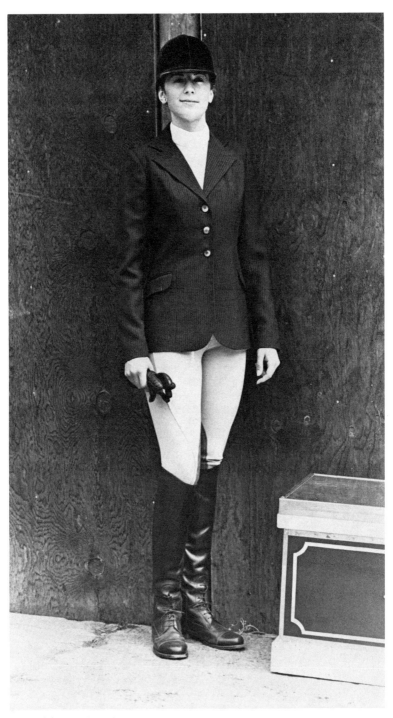

Dressed for the show ring.

ness, which may be fastened for jumping classes
and then removed for flat classes. Girls with long
hair should buy a hat large enough to accommo-
date all that hair once it is tucked out of the way
under the hat.

Jacket   Riding jackets should be dark in color and fit to
            allow plenty of room to bend your elbows and
            move your shoulders.

Shirts   Boys should wear a white shirt with an appro-
            priate tie. Girls wear "rat-catchers," a shirt with a
            detachable, velcro-fastened collar called a choker.
            These shirts come in a variety of colors, with or
            without sleeves. The choker may be mono-
            grammed with your initials, or a small pin may be
            worn.

Breeches   Young children often wear jodhpurs, with jodh-
or   pur garters or straps worn around the legs just
Jodhpurs   below the knee. Older children and adults wear
            breeches. Both come in four-way stretch fabrics
            that are virtually indestructible and superbly com-
            fortable and that will stretch with you as you
            grow. They come in beige, gray, tan, brick, ca-
            nary, and white.

Boots   These may be black dress or field boots. Boots
            may be made-to-measure (lovely but very expen-
            sive), ready-made (of medium expense), or of in-
            expensive rubber. Ideally boots should fit the leg
            snugly without gaping at the tops and should ex-
            tend up as close to the knee as possible, since
            they tend to drop when broken in. Children wear-
            ing jodhpurs wear jodhpur boots, though leather
            lace-up shoes are also correct for the beginner.

Gloves   Dark leather or nylon riding gloves. Make sure
                they fit your hand comfortably across the knuck-
                les when your hand is in a fist.

Show Tack You may not be able to afford that super French
saddle you've been daydreaming about or that fancy double-
stitched raised show bridle, but you *can* clean your tack so that
it looks good and enhances your horse's show appearance.
You may not own the most expensive tack, but all that really
matters is that what you have is clean, neat, and in good repair.
Your bit and stirrup irons should dazzle the spectators with
their brilliance; your saddle pad should be freshly laundered;
and all the leather should be freshly saddle-soaped so that it
gleams. Here are a few of the details that make the difference
between a well-turned out horse and one that looks sloppy.

- Make sure your bridle is adjusted properly and evenly,
  with the cavesson snug and all straps of the bridle
  neatly in their respective keepers so that they are not
  flapping about.
- Are your stirrups the right size for your feet? Children
  generally need a smaller stirrup than adults. Have you
  remembered to scrub the mud out of your stirrup
  treads?
- Are your stirrup leathers the right length for your legs?
  Leathers come in several different lengths, and if a
  child uses an adult leather, then there is often an excess
  of leather hanging behind the rider's leg. This looks
  untidy.
- Make sure your saddle pad is placed squarely under the
  saddle so that an equal amount of white pad shows all
  around the saddle. Pads put on hurriedly have a ten-
  dency to work loose and be lopsided once you are in
  the ring. This is messy.
- Remember to tighten your girth.

Horse and rider neatly turned out and ready for the ring.

The same horse and rider, but what a difference. The rider's hair is an untidy mess, her jacket is unbuttoned, and her boots need a polish. As for the horse, the cavesson is crooked, the braids are falling out, and the pad is askew. No wonder the mare looks moody.

Your Horse's Show Appearance Your horse's appearance for the show ring is accomplished in four phases.

Phase 1: As a result of a good feeding program coupled with a regular worming and vaccination schedule, your horse should present a pleasing, well-fleshed, and healthy appearance together with a shining coat. Make a note to have your horse reshod if necessary at least a week prior to the show.

Phase 2: The day before the show, your horse should have a shampoo. Pay particular attention to any white stars or stockings. Put a sheet on afterward to keep him clean. It helps to bandage white legs to ensure that they stay white. Next trim your horse with clippers around his jaw, muzzle, ears, and fetlocks, and give him a small bridle-path behind his ears (the width of three fingers is an ideal measurement). Last but not

Make a note to have your horse re-shod if necessary at least a week before the show.

least, be sure to put your horse to bed early the night before the show so that he can thoroughly relax and eat properly.

Phase 3:   Early on the morning of show day, you should get up in plenty of time to allow your horse to eat breakfast. Then braid his mane and tail if necessary. Remember to allow more time than you think you will need.

Phase 4:   Once at the show, your horse should be groomed, his feet cleaned out, and his hooves oiled. This is the time to straighten out any of the braids that may have become crooked and to brush out the horse's tail. Then it's time to tack up, paying particular attention to all those small but important details mentioned previously.

CHAPTER **6**

SHOWING

RIDING IS THE only sport where a human and an animal compete as a single unit. The would-be competitor should remember that showing is very much a horse-and-rider *team* effort. When you show, each partner of the team must cooperate with the other for the team to be successful. This holds true even though various classes are judged differently. For instance, in an equitation class, the judge will be evaluating your riding skills at the various gaits. However, if your horse decides to buck in all the corners or runs off with you in the canter, then you will hardly be able to concentrate on your riding technique. The judge will see an ill-mannered horse with a rider obviously having difficulty controlling the situa-

Showing.

tion, and she will probably mark your equitation score down accordingly. So remember, whatever the class, the outcome depends entirely upon a team effort between you and your horse.

Since most shows are run in accordance with the rules of the American Horse Shows Association, Inc. (598 Madison Avenue, New York, New York 10022), the prospective show rider should join this organization. You will receive a copy of the A.H.S.A. Rule Book, which lists all the rules, class descriptions, and various tests plus the names of all recognized judges. In the meantime, here is a rundown of each of the classes and a brief description of what will be expected of you and your equine partner.

Hunt Seat Equitation, Flat   In equitation classes the judge will be looking at you to evaluate how well you influence your horse at the walk, trot, and canter. Although you are the partner being scored in this class, hopefully your horse will cooperate by changing gaits when asked, by picking up the correct leads, and by bending in all the corners. It is up to you to ride on the correct diagonal at the trot. Should your horse pick up the incorrect lead, you must immediately change to the correct one. In all flat classes you will be asked to walk, trot, and canter in both directions of the ring. In larger shows you may be asked to perform an individual equitation test (taken from the A.H.S.A. Rule Book). Don't panic. Listen carefully to the judge's instructions. Stay calm and concentrate. Then do your best.

Equitation over Fences   Once again, the judge will be looking at your equitation style and position, only this time you ride over a course of fences. He will evaluate if you get the correct striding between each jump, if you change leads appropriately, and so on. At the end of the class, the judge usually calls back the four riders he thought were best and asks each to perform a

Equitation over fences. In this class the judge will be evaluating your style and position as you ride the course of fences.

test individually. You may be asked to trot certain fences, ride fences without stirrups, or stop between fences and back up. Once again, listen carefully to the judge's instructions and then concentrate totally as you perform.

Working Hunters under Saddle   This is a flat class, and the judge will be noting how well your horse moves and performs as he walks, trots, canters, and hand gallops in each direction of the ring.

Working Hunter Hack   This class is judged both on the flat and over two fences. Once again, the horse is being judged on his way of going and manners. Points are given both for the flat work and the two fences.

Working Hunters   Here the judge looks for an even hunting pace between the fences and the horse's style over the fence, his way of going, and his manners. At the end of the class, the judge chooses which horses she likes. These riders dismount (and run up their stirrups) and trot their horses into the arena before the judge so that she can see whether or not each horse is sound. In the event that a horse is lame, he is disqualified and the horse next in line moves up a place.

Jumpers   All that matters in jumpers is that the horse clear each fence of the course and not stop in between. He is then scored accordingly. Style has no bearing on the outcome. A description of how each jumper class is to be scored is always given in the show prize list and can then be looked up in the A.H.S.A. Rule Book.

Class Categories   To give each competitor a fair chance in the show ring, classes are often split into various categories so that beginners do not have to compete against seasoned riders. For instance, most junior classes are divided into age groups.

Working Hunters. Here the judge looks at the horse's style over the fences, his way of going, his pace, and his manners.

Jumpers. In Jumpers, the horse must clear each fence of the course and not stop in-between. He is scored on a penalty basis accordingly. Notice that this jumper is wearing splint and bell boots to protect his legs.

There are classes for amateur adults, and these too are sometimes divided into age groups. There are maiden classes for
horses and/or riders who have never won a first. There are
novice classes for horses and/or riders who have not won three
firsts. Limit classes are for horses and/or riders who have not
won six firsts. Open classes are open to everyone, including
the professionals. There are green classes for inexperienced
horses and even pre-green classes for kindergarten equines.
Working hunter classes can also be divided by the rider's age
and given all sorts of additional tricky titles such as any weight,
regular, handy, small, and large. Championship classes are
often called stake classes. In the breed shows, classes are divided by the sex and age of the horses being shown.

What to Do upon Arrival at the Show   Rule number one is to
arrive at the show grounds in plenty of time to:

- Unload your horse, tie him up to the trailer or van, and
  hang up his hay net and water bucket.
- Sweep out any manure from the trailer. This allows the
  floor to dry during the day and discourages flies.
- Pick up your competitor number at the show entry
  desk.
- Visit the bathroom if necessary.
- Groom and tack up your horse.
- Dress in your show clothes, pull on your boots, do your
  hair, and adjust your hat correctly.
- Attach your number. Tip: A black shoelace long
  enough to go around your waist makes an excellent
  number-attacher. (In between shows, the shoelace can
  be conveniently kept in your riding jacket pocket.)
- Warm up your horse for the first class.

Remember, all these chores will take you far longer to accomplish than you imagine. Nothing is more nerve-racking

Attaching your show number. Here's a tip. A black shoelace long enough to go around your waist makes an excellent number-attacher and may be kept in your jacket pocket in-between shows.

than to arrive late for the show and have to rush madly about trying to get ready in time for that first class. It is easier to avoid this frustration by allowing sufficient time for all your pre-first-class preparations.

Warming Up   Once you are mounted, it is time to warm up your horse. How much warm-up depends largely on your particular horse. This is where your own common sense comes into play. If your horse is spirited and needs working down, then you must allow sufficient time to get the bucks out, even longeing him if necessary. If, on the other hand, your horse tends to be lazy and you want to save his energy for the classes ahead, then only a five-minute warm-up may be necessary.

Warm-up areas at shows are invariably small and crowded, often resembling a cavalry combat zone where what seems like dozens of horses charge from all directions at one or two schooling fences. It is prudent to ride defensively "with the traffic" around the perimeter of this madness, working your horse at the walk, trot, and canter until he is listening to you. If your first class is over fences, then line up with the flow of traffic and trot a few crossrails before cantering low verticals. Don't overdo the jump schooling. The chaotic atmosphere of the warm-up area is distracting and horses find it hard to concentrate. However, try to jump a couple of fences that are the same height as those in the class, so that your horse is as well prepared as possible for the course ahead.

Riding Competitively in the Show Ring In a nutshell, riding competitively means *maximizing your good points and minimizing your bad ones.*

To be successful in flat classes you must be seen by the judge. Remember, he can only judge what he can see, and if there are thirty or more riders circling around him on the rail, he is only going to be able to catch a momentary glimpse of each competitor. Therefore, it is imperative that the glimpses he catches of you be good ones and that you and your horse present as perfect a picture as possible (which is why so much emphasis was placed on your appearance). The trick is to find a spot on the rail by yourself so that the judge will have an opportunity to get a good look at you. To achieve this, you may have to circle or even cross the ring to place yourself in the most advantageous position possible *before* you reach the

Warming up. This excellent warm-up area is unusually quiet and uncrowded. Warm-up areas at most shows are small, crowded, and chaotic.

judge's line of vision. Whatever you do, don't circle around the judge. Most judges find this ploy irritating (and quite frightening) and tend to ignore such a rider. Most judges prefer competitors to ride on the rail if at all possible.

Because each class is judged differently—the judge evaluates the *rider* in equitation classes and the *horse* in hunter and under saddle classes—it is important to realize that each class must be ridden with these specifics in mind. Therefore, in equitation classes, you must make every effort to make your riding appear smooth and correct. Any annoying gaits or habits your horse may have which could possibly affect your equitation must somehow be minimized, and your good points highlighted. For instance, if your horse has a long-strided trot that tends to throw you too far out of the saddle, making your equitation appear a little rough, then slow down with as much finesse as you can *before* you approach the judge's line of vision. In this way, your trot work appears smoother. If your horse makes you nervous because he is consistently naughty about picking up the correct canter lead, then maneuver yourself into a herd of other riders when asked for the canter depart, where any mistakes you make won't be quite as visible. Then, when you are safely on the correct lead, you can position yourself in a good spot on the rail and canter serenely before the judge.

In under saddle classes when the judge is evaluating the horse's performance, again maximize your horse's good points and try to minimize his poorer qualities. If he has a mincing trot, but a smooth, rhythmic canter, then by all means show the judge the lovely canter to maximum effect. But when you are asked to trot, extend the trot (by pushing with your seat and applying additional leg pressure) as much as possible while positioning your horse discreetly behind other riders. If your horse tends to buck and play in the corners when asked for a hand gallop, then bring him back a little as tactfully as possible every time you approach a corner to avoid behavior problems that might be scored against you.

When competing in fence classes, get to the ring in plenty of time to watch other competitors ride the course. This will give you an idea of the striding, how to ride the course, what combinations to watch out for, and where to best make the turns. Watch how the horses handle the footing in the ring. Are there any deep spots where the footing has become heavy and where the horses tend to lose forward momentum? Are there any slick spots due to overwatering where you may have to exercise extreme caution? Watching other riders compete gives you an opportunity to learn which trouble spots to avoid and how to best tackle the course.

When riding a course of fences, it is not quite as easy to minimize errors, because you are alone in the ring and all eyes are on you. How you handle mistakes depends to a great extent upon the gravity of the offense. Knock-downs and refusals are major faults, and chances are that with a mistake of this magnitude you have blown the class anyway. This being the case, you may as well use the remaining fences to school your horse, making sure that he does not refuse again.

But there are lesser errors such as lead changes, incorrect striding, cross-firing, and erratic pace that you can minimize with your own riding finesse. For instance, suppose your horse is having a very nice round but suddenly puts in an extra stride down a line of three. Do you show your displeasure at the mistake, grimly setting your mouth and pushing (with the aid of a whip) for the correct striding for the remainder of the course? No. You try to pretend the mistake didn't happen, that it was simply a figment of everyone's imagination. You concentrate on the positive aspects of your nice round and, mustering all your calm confidence, try to finish the course as you started it. This attitude will very often result not only in a halfway decent round but with a ribbon as a bonus. Why? Because you didn't allow the error to rattle you. You coped with it in a positive way, with the result that you and your horse pulled yourselves together and regained your mutual composure.

Whatever the class, try to appear calm and confident no matter how shaky you feel inside. If you look grim and anxious, you will convey your anxiety to the judge (not to mention your horse) who may wonder what is wrong with your animal to cause you so much concern. Relax and enjoy yourself.

CHAPTER 7

LEASING OR
SPONSORING HORSES

YOU MAY BE one of those horsemen who loves working with the animal, taking lessons, riding on the trails, or showing, but for one reason or another cannot actually *own* a horse. It may be that you can afford to keep a horse, but can't afford to buy one. (Or perhaps you are a beginning rider, and you want to find out just how much commitment is involved before actually making the plunge into the responsibilities of horse ownership.) Fortunately, you can enjoy the pleasures of equine companionship without the necessity of ownership, thanks to the increasing popularity of leasing or sponsoring.

What Is Leasing or Sponsoring?　Leasing or sponsoring a horse means making a contract with the horse's owner to be responsible for all, or part, of the horse's board, shoeing, and vet bills. Sometimes the owner wants to share the riding privileges with the sponsor, so a schedule must be worked out dividing the riding time and expenses between the two parties. Whatever the agreement, the terms should be mutually agreed upon in writing, and both parties should sign the contract.

What Are Your Responsibilities?　If you sponsor or lease a horse, it will be your responsibility to maintain the horse in a

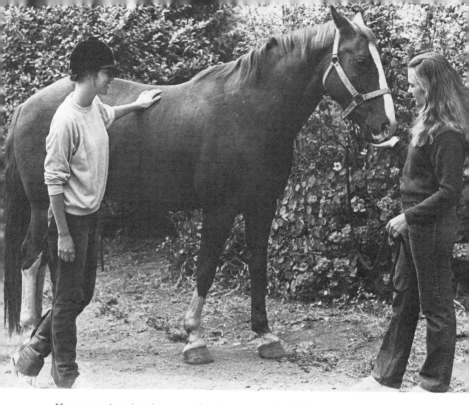

You can enjoy the pleasures of equine companionship by sponsoring or leasing a horse.

sound, unblemished condition and to return the horse to his owner in the same condition. All intelligent horse owners realize that horses are subject to occasional accidents and breakdowns. However, it is the sponsor's responsibility to ensure that any such accident or breakdown is not a result of his negligence. If you decide to sponsor a horse, you will have to know enough about horses to ride and groom him properly, make sure he is housed suitably, recognize any signs of illness or disability, worm and vaccinate him regularly, and shoe him as necessary. Unless it is specified otherwise in your contract with the owner, if you plan to show or compete with the horse, you must notify the owner and obtain permission first. If the horse is particularly valuable, it may be advisable to take out an equine insurance policy on his life. It is a good rule of thumb if you are sponsoring a horse to treat the horse's owner and the horse as you would wish to be treated if the roles were reversed.

What Are the Benefits of Sponsoring? Despite all the responsibilities of sponsoring (most of which you would face anyway if you owned the animal), the benefits of the arrangement are manyfold. For instance, it may be possible for you to sponsor and compete with a top-quality show horse that you couldn't afford to buy. Sponsoring allows you the freedom of choosing a horse trained in the discipline you are particularly interested in, such as dressage, hunting, jumping, or simply pleasure riding. As you move up the equitation ladder, you won't have to face the difficult task of selling one horse so that you can purchase a more accomplished and more expensive animal. If you move frequently, you won't have to concern yourself with the high cost of moving and relocating your horse. You simply stop leasing in one location and find a new horse when you settle in your new home. There is no need to own a horse in order to be a successful horseman.

How Do You Go about Leasing? You can advertise in your local newspaper or horse magazine. You can visit boarding, training, and breeding stables and leave notices on their notice boards. List your experience as a rider (and don't exaggerate your abilities, for you will be quickly and embarrassingly found out), and how much time and money you have to spend on riding.

When you find some prospective candidates, make an appointment with the owners and try out each horse. In each case ask yourself if the animal is suitable for your riding needs. If you only want to ride on the trails on a Sunday afternoon, you won't need to sponsor an expensive show hunter.

Try out several horses if possible before you decide which one is the most suited to you. Then ask yourself if you are compatible with the owner. Do you agree on the type and quality of care the horse should receive and how the horse should be ridden and handled? Getting along with the owner is almost as important as getting along with the horse.

Equipment You Will Need You may not own your horse, but there is no reason why you can't have your own equipment. If properly looked after, these items will last for years. It is a satisfying feeling to know that no matter where or what you ride, your own familiar equipment goes along with you.

Whichever riding discipline you are interested in, you will need riding clothes: a hard hat to protect your head and boots and breeches (or shotguns) to prevent your legs from being chafed. If you are interested in showing, you will also need a suitable riding jacket and gloves. The most important item you should consider purchasing is a saddle. Although owners are willing to allow their horses to be leased out, very few will loan their tack. A good-quality saddle is almost a must for the would-be sponsor. Almost as important is a bridle, with perhaps several different bits to suit a variety of horses. Last but not least, a tack box containing the necessary grooming tools and a few first-aid supplies is necessary.

How To Sponsor Out Your Horse You may have a horse for which you wish to find a sponsor. Perhaps you are going off to college or have a job, and suddenly you don't have time to spend with your horse. But you can't bring yourself to sell him. Finding a sponsor may well be your answer.

Advertise in your local newspaper or horse magazine and carefully screen any prospective sponsors. Then allow the most likely prospects to visit and try out your horse. Carefully evaluate how each treats the animal, noting whether proper grooming procedures are followed, how each person tacks up and handles your horse, and how each potential sponsor rides. Study each applicant's attitude to your horse. Is the animal treated with care and respect or simply regarded as a piece of equipment?

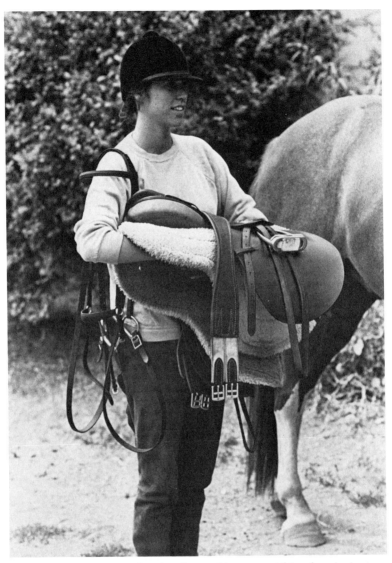

You may not own the horse, but there is something very satisfying about having your own equipment when you sponsor a horse. You will need a hard hat, boots and breeches (or chaps), and, if possible, your own saddle and bridle.

When you have found a candidate who looks like he'll be a loving parent to your horse, you should both sign an agreement specifying the care and use of the animal. Make sure you have visiting rights, so that you can reassure yourself that your horse is happy and cared for.

CHAPTER 8

BREEDING YOUR OWN

MOST PEOPLE WHO own a mare daydream about breeding her one day and raising the perfect offspring. However, in order to realize this happy state, the amateur breeder should cast aside all those romantic notions about horse breeding and carefully research what is actually involved. There are as many good reasons *not* to breed as there are to breed, and the wise owner should educate herself thoroughly before doing anything.

One important factor to consider is cost. It is no use deluding yourself that you will acquire your dream horse for the price of the stud fee. By the time you have bred your mare and raised the offspring to an age when he can be ridden, your cash outlay will at least equal and perhaps exceed what you would pay for a similar horse on the open market. On the other hand, you have the enormous satisfaction of knowing your young horse's parentage and how he was raised. You don't need to worry that your three-year-old may have been asked to do too much too soon, or that he may have incurred injuries that don't show yet.

Should Your Mare Be Bred?   The first question the potential horse breeder should ask is whether or not his mare should be bred. Too often backyard mares are bred not for their performance record or bloodlines but because the owner thought it would be cute for the mare to have a baby. Or because the

Most people who own a mare daydream about breeding her and raising the perfect offspring.

You probably won't save any money by raising your own foal, but you will have the enormous satisfaction of knowing your horse's parentage and how it was raised.

Great care should be taken to choose a stallion with good formation and a kindly disposition.

mare had broken down and the owner thought, why not breed her? Or because the owner thought he could make money raising horses and selling them. None of these reasons alone is sufficient to take on the expense and responsibility of raising a foal. The horse breeder should attempt to breed only if the mare has *several* of the following qualities:

- A pleasant disposition
- Good conformation
- A worthy performance record
- No unsoundness problems (unless caused by accident)
- Bloodlines worth continuing

Choosing a Stallion The purpose of breeding should be to pass along desirable qualities of each parent to the offspring. Since no horse is perfect, the potential breeder should look for virtues in one parent that will complement the faults of the other. For instance, if your quarter horse mare has small feet, you should use a stallion, perhaps of another breed, with particularly well-conformed feet in the hopes that the foal will inherit them, or at least end up with larger feet than his dam's.

Particular attention should be paid to the qualities and characteristics of each breed so that you can use proven traits to your advantage when breeding. Suppose you have a docile Morgan mare who has been a splendid trail horse. You would like a colt that is a larger version of her, one that you could trail ride and maybe show as a hunter. To obtain the increased height you would have to choose a breed larger than the Morgan, perhaps a quarter horse or maybe a Thoroughbred. Carefully research the qualities and characteristics of each breed. Thoroughbreds, although elegant, tend to be highly strung and nervous, having been bred for centuries to run fast. Quarter horses are generally more easygoing animals with well-muscled bodies and pleasant temperaments. Once you have chosen your breed and finally narrowed down your choice of stallion, ask to see some of his get (offspring). This will give you an idea how your foal will develop and grow, so that you will know what to expect. There is one last consideration—temperament. Does the stallion have a pleasant disposition? Good or bad temperament is nearly always inherited by the offspring, and disposition is one of the few things that cannot be changed in the horse.

Once you have firmly decided upon the stallion and the stud fee, the stallion owner will probably ask you to sign a breeding contract. The breeder usually will ask for a booking fee with the balance of the stud fee due and payable upon the live birth of the foal. There will be boarding expenses incurred while your mare is at the breeding farm waiting to be bred, and vet bills for the prebreeding checkup and the subsequent confirmation of her pregnancy.

Heat Cycles and Gestation   Mares come into season (or heat) every two to three weeks during the early spring and summer months and taper off during the winter months. When a mare is in season, she appears to urinate excessively and will usually kick or squeal when approached by another horse. Once bred, the gestation period (the length of time between conception and the birth of the foal) lasts for eleven months. To give the new foal the advantage of spring grass and warm weather, breeders try to time the mare's breeding so that she will give birth in the spring. For instance, a mare bred in April will be expected to drop her foal in March of the following year.

Breeding the Mare   Each time the mare comes into season, she stays in heat for approximately five days. It is during this period that she is willing to allow the stallion to service her. At a breeding farm, a veterinarian will probably examine the mare prior to the breeding to ascertain her physical condition and whether she is ready to ovulate. During this heat period, the breeder may decide to have the stallion service the mare on several occasions. Several weeks after the service, the vet will again examine the mare to see if she is pregnant. Once the mare is in foal, she will not come into season again until about ten days after the birth of her offspring. This season is called the foaling heat.

The Pregnant Mare   Most healthy mares may be ridden sensibly up until about three months prior to the birth, though the mare should not be overtaxed. She should be on a well-balanced, high-protein feeding program supplemented with vitamins. If you are not sure what your mare's diet should consist of, ask your vet to give you a program to suit her needs. Your vet will probably also want your mare wormed regularly to keep her as parasite-free as possible.

Apart from no longer coming into season, there will be very little external evidence for many months that your mare is in foal. In the last five months, her belly will gradually start to distend. If you are fortunate you may be lucky enough to occasionally see the foal moving inside the mare. Shortly before the mare is to foal, her udder (also called her bag) will swell and milk will start to drip out. This is called waxing. With some mares this is an indication that the birth is imminent; with others it may be days or even weeks away. When the mare actually starts to foal, her contractions are so strong that the arrival of the foal usually takes less than thirty minutes. The birth is almost invariably at night. Should the labor continue more than thirty minutes, call your veterinarian immediately.

Where to Foal   Ideally your mare should foal in a flat, green pasture surrounded by safe fencing (not barbed wire). The mare should be alone or with one or two other mares provided they are gentle and the pasture is large. Should your mare live in a large herd situation, she should be separated from the other horses until after she has foaled to prevent possible harassment or injury to her foal (which sadly happens all too often).

If your mare is to foal in a paddock, make sure the area is large and spotlessly clean with safe fencing, including a rail at ground level to prevent the foal from rolling out under the fence. Spread a bed of clean straw in the center of the paddock to encourage your mare to foal there, away from the fence. Use straw rather than shavings for bedding at foaling time. Shavings can sometimes be inhaled by the newborn and may possibly cause an infection of the mare's birth canal. If you plan to use a stall, it should be very large, clean, and well bedded with deep straw.

Foaling   Watching the birth of a foal is an exciting and touching experience. You have to be extremely lucky to see it happen, because most mares have a knack for waiting until they are alone before dropping the foal. In a normal foaling, the mare will pace around nervously, sometimes kicking her belly and sometimes lying down for short periods. Most mares foal while lying down, but a few prefer to stand. The first thing you will see is a bubble of membrane protruding from the vagina (the water bag that housed the unborn foal), followed by two little front hooves and the foal's nose. After a few more powerful contractions, the foal slithers completely out.

After the foal is born, allow the umbilical cord to break naturally, so that the foal receives as much nourishing blood as possible from the placenta (which is still within the mare at this point). Then dab some iodine on the foal's navel, to prevent the possibility of infection. The mare usually stands almost immediately after the birth. The foal should attempt to stand within a few minutes. His first attempts will be quite wobbly and he will probably fall down several times before eventually succeeding. Once up, he will head for his mother's udder for some milk. This first nursing is very important because the mare's first milk (called colostrum) contains antibodies that immunize the foal against bacterial infection.

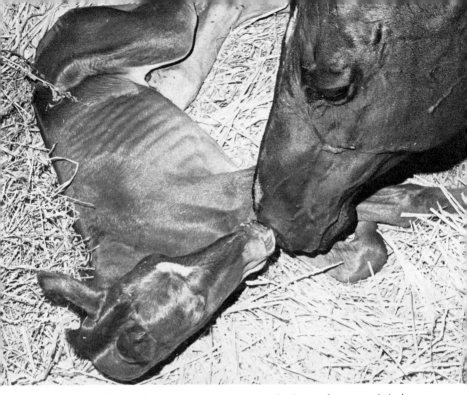

Watching the birth of a foal is an exciting event. You also have to be extremely lucky because most mares seem to wait until they are alone to give birth.

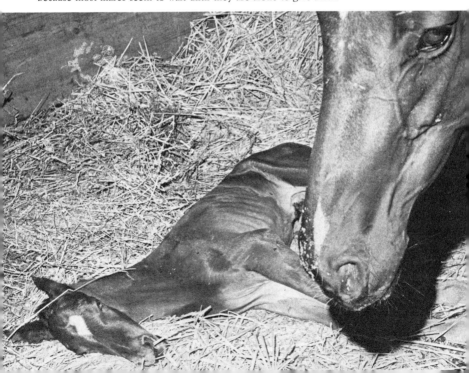

The owner should keep a close watch on the mare to make sure that all is well, and that the placenta (a large red, blue, and brown membrane that nourished the unborn foal) has been passed. Your vet may want to examine this placenta, so place it in a plastic bag and store it somewhere cool until the vet arrives. Should the placenta fail to pass within five or six hours, call your vet. A retained placenta can cause infection, founder, and even the death of the mare.

After the birth, remove any soiled bedding and feed the mare a wholesome bran mash. She deserves it.

The arrival of the new foal is a magical happening.

CHAPTER *9*

RAISING THE FOAL

THE ARRIVAL OF a new foal is a magical happening, with everyone hanging over the fence to marvel at the baby's wobbly antics and chuckle as he clumsily nudges his dam for more milk. After the initial excitement and within twenty-four hours of the birth, it is advisable to have your veterinarian give the foal a physical. This will probably include a shot of antibiotics to prevent infection and tetanus antitoxin to prevent tetanus (lockjaw). The vet will want to examine the mare at the same time, to make sure that she too came through the birth with flying colors.

For the first two or three weeks after foaling, the mare and foal should be kept in a large paddock or small pasture by themselves so that they can get to know each other. This will also give the foal a chance to thoroughly perfect his nursing and running techniques. After that, if both mother and offspring are healthy and the weather is good, they can be turned out in a large pasture with a few other gentle horses.

Feeding the Mare and Foal Just as the mare was fed a high-protein and well-balanced diet while she was in foal, it is equally important that she receive a nourishing diet now that she is nursing her offspring. A lactating mare can produce

For the first two or three weeks after foaling, the mare and foal should be kept in a small paddock or pasture by themselves.

Alone with the mare, the foal gets to perfect his nursing technique.

If mother and offspring are healthy and the weather is good, they can be turned out in a large pasture.

It is important that the mare receive a nourishing diet when she is nursing. This mare is nursing twin foals, a rarity in the horse world.

as much as five gallons of milk a day, but in order to do so she must receive additional alfalfa hay and grain. Otherwise, she will quickly start to lose weight and condition. The foal too will soon start to nibble at his mother's grain ration. Before long, depending on the breed, weight, and where he is kept, he will require additional grain to supplement his mother's milk and the grazing. Some breeders like to build a "creep" in the corner of the field or paddock. This is a small pen only the foal can enter where he can eat the grain ration at leisure throughout the day. Fresh water and a trace mineral salt block should be available to the mare and foal at all times. To be absolutely sure you are feeding your new family correctly, it is advisable to consult your veterinarian to get a feeding program that suits their individual needs.

Preventive Health Care for the Foal   It is very important to set up a vaccination program with your veterinarian. Your new foal can be immunized against a host of unpleasant viral and bacterial diseases such as tetanus, eastern and western encephalitis, influenza, rhinopneumonitis, strangles, and rabies. You should also ask your vet to regularly worm the foal to keep him as parasite-free as possible.

Handling the Foal   The foal's education begins shortly after birth. It is worthwhile to spend some time on a daily or weekly basis gently, but firmly, handling him. As a consequence of this, he will grow up accepting human authority as a natural part of his life. This will save you a great deal of work later on when the horse is much larger and stronger.

The first step is to fit the horse with a small halter and lead him around following his mother. If he balks—and he probably will—you can place a rope around his rump to help persuade him to move forward. Get him used to being groomed. Start by stroking him, and then run the brush over his neck and shoulder until he accepts grooming as a part of his daily routine. Foals love to be scratched around the neck and rump

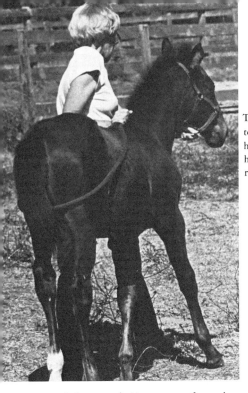

The first step in a foal's education is to fit him with a small halter and lead him around following his mother. If he balks, place a rope around his rump . . .

. . . to help persuade him to move forward.

area, and it is possible to mesmerize them into an almost trancelike state with a good itch. Remember to use this tip whenever you need to pacify the foal, such as when the vet has to give him a shot. Regularly pick up all four of his feet and clean out his tiny hooves so that he gets used to the idea of having his feet and legs handled. This will really help your farrier later on.

Some foals are more docile than others and as a result are easier to handle than their more spirited brothers and sisters. With patience and perseverance, all foals should be used to the halter, leading, grooming, and feet cleaning by the time they are six months old and ready to wean.

Weaning the Foal   When the foal is about six months old, he is usually taken away from his mother. This process is called weaning. The mare is allowed to dry up, and perhaps go back to being a riding horse again. The foal learns to make new friends. There are a couple of different ways for the horseman to successfully accomplish weaning. Obviously, the least stressful method should be used. Whatever the method, the mare's grain should be withdrawn approximately one week prior to the weaning, so that her milk production is lowered.

If there are several mares and foals in a field, the mares can gradually be removed one at a time over a period of several days. In this way, each motherless foal has the company of the other colts and fillies, and they can console one another. The foal's grain and alfalfa ration should then be increased to make up for the loss of the mare's milk. The fencing of the pasture must be safe and strong, and there should always be someone around during the weaning period to ensure that none of the foals gets into trouble.

Another weaning method is to place mother and foal in adjoining paddocks, where they can still see each other but the foal can no longer nurse. It helps if another gentle horse or foal is put in with the youngster to keep him company and to

When foals are about six months old, they are usually weaned from their dams.

help reduce the anguish should his mother be taken out for rides occasionally. Again, the foal's grain and hay rations should be increased to make up for the milk loss.

The mare is uncomfortably engorged with milk for a few days after the initial separation, but she will soon start to dry up. The main point is to try to make the weaning process as humane as possible for both mare and foal.

Gelding the Colt   Somewhere between eight and eighteen months of age, the male foal is usually castrated. Exactly when he should be gelded depends on his physical development and whether or not he is a nuisance to the mares and fillies when he is out in a pasture. Most veterinarians perform the operation while the animal is standing. The procedure takes only a few minutes. The colt is given a sedative, and then each testicle is injected with a local anesthetic. The testicles are then removed and the spermatic cord is crushed to prevent hemorrhage.

Most colts do not react adversely to the surgery. They often

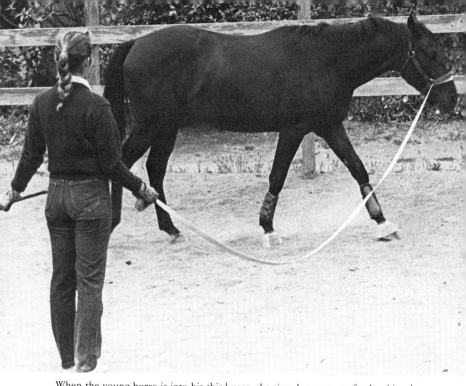

When the young horse is into his third year, the time has come to further his education by teaching him, among other things, to longe . . .

. . . and load in a trailer.

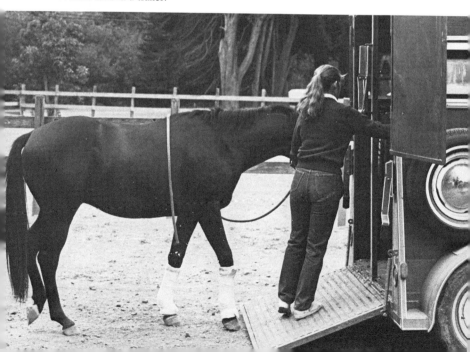

return to normal eating and behaving as soon as the effects of the anesthetic have worn off. Because the wound drains well, very little after care is necessary, other than making sure the colt is well exercised. Should he run a temperature or go off his feed, then the vet should be called immediately.

Early Training of the Young Horse   For the first two years of the young horse's life, he should be allowed to run free in pasture, interacting with other horses. During this interval, the horseman should routinely worm, vaccinate, and trim the colt's feet, at the same time handling him on a frequent basis so that he remains used to human contact and authority.

When the young horse is well into his third year, the time has come to further his education by teaching him to longe, stand while tied, and load in a trailer. He should also have his feet shod for the first time if necessary, get used to having various parts of his body clipped, and should be longed while saddled and bridled. In this way, when the day arrives when your three-year-old can finally be ridden, he will be as prepared for the occasion as you are.

CHAPTER 10

FIRST AID AND EMERGENCY CARE

HORSES ARE SUBJECT to occasional injuries and illnesses, and every horseman should know how to recognize symptoms and learn what should be done before the veterinarian arrives. This information might one day help save a horse's life or at least prevent permanent injury to the animal. In an emergency situation, try to remain calm so that you can accurately assess the problem and relay this information to your vet. And while you are waiting for him to arrive, calm and reassure the horse.

To refresh your memory, the horse's temperature, pulse, and respiration rates are:

Temperature: The average temperature of the horse is 99–101°F (38–39°C).

Pulse: The horse's pulse should beat approximately forty times a minute when the animal is at rest.

Respiration: The average horse takes between eight and sixteen breaths a minute.

Colic This is definitely an equine medical emergency and can result from several different causes. Internal parasites, a recent change in feed, too much grain, strenuous exercise too soon after feeding, and even the chewing of wood or rubber fencing can cause colic. The symptoms are: obvious internal distress, with the horse frequently kicking and looking at his belly; rolling and thrashing about; sweating on the neck and flanks. *Before* you call your vet, check the following and write down the results:

> Take the temperature, pulse, and respiration rates.
> Is your horse passing manure?
> How is the animal behaving?
> Has anything unusual happened in the horse's routine or feeding program?

Now call your vet. While you wait for him to arrive, walk the horse gently around and try to prevent him from rolling. Do not feed or medicate the horse unless your vet has specifically asked you to.

Eye Injuries or Diseases   Don't try to treat or medicate the injured eye yourself. It is hard for the lay person to know the extent of the problem, and incorrect treatment could cause further damage to the eye. If possible, put the horse in a darkened stall and call your vet. Eye injuries or diseases should always be treated immediately. Don't wait. If you don't have a dark stall available, tie a patch over the injured eye to keep light and dust from causing further irritation until help arrives.

Hemorrhage   This type of injury can be caused by a kick or a cut. Suddenly there is a frightening amount of blood every-

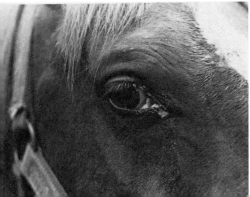

Eye injuries or diseases should be treated immediately. Call your veterinarian.

where. If an artery has been severed, bright red blood spurts out in the rhythm of the heartbeat. This type of hemorrhage occurs most commonly to the legs because the arteries are close to the surface. To control the bleeding, pressure must be applied immediately to the wound. Make a thick pad (any clean towel, sanitary napkin, or padded cotton wrap will do) and, using a track bandage, wrap the injury as firmly as you can. Do not use a tourniquet; you may cause more harm than good. Call your vet immediately so that he can repair the damaged artery or vein and treat the wound.

Lameness in General Lameness can be caused by numerous things: by injury; by the loss of a shoe; by a foreign object in the foot; by disease; by bruising; by straining muscles, tendons, and ligaments; and by fractures. If your horse is lame, and you can't immediately find the cause (such as a rock or nail in the hoof, or a lost shoe), call your vet. It may not be an emergency situation, but any lameness should be diagnosed as quickly as possible so that the appropriate treatment can begin. If your horse goes lame for a reason you cannot determine when you are out riding, dismount and lead the animal home.

Sprains If your horse is suddenly lame and you find there is heat, pain, and swelling in the area behind the cannon bone or around the fetlock joint, very probably your horse has

Lameness can be caused by a wide variety of different reasons, including a rock wedged in the bottom of the foot.

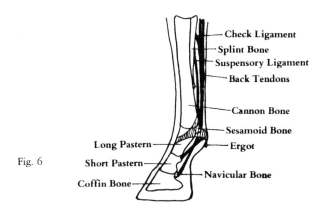

Check Ligament
Splint Bone
Suspensory Ligament
Back Tendons

Cannon Bone
Sesamoid Bone

Long Pastern
Ergot

Fig. 6

Short Pastern

Coffin Bone
Navicular Bone

sprained a tendon, a check ligament, or a suspensory ligament (See Fig. 6). Hose the area for half an hour with cold water or apply ice (those soft, gel-type ice packs are excellent for wrapping around a horse's legs). Then apply a support bandage to the area and call your vet. He will be able to diagnose the cause and severity of the sprain and will probably prescribe complete rest and hot and cold treatments accompanied by an anti-inflammatory drug. In very severe cases, your vet may decide to apply a soft cast to the affected leg to ensure complete rest.

Fractures   If you suspect your horse's leg is fractured, do not move the animal any more than absolutely necessary. Try to immobilize the fractured leg by applying a "pillow splint." Take an ordinary bed pillow and wrap it lengthwise around the injured leg. Wrap track bandages firmly around the pillow until the leg is totally immobilized. Do not administer any medication. Call your vet immediately, then return to your horse and remain calm and reassuring. While you are waiting, apply a support wrap to the partner leg, as this leg now has to carry the weight of both legs. And take heart, many horses these days do recover from fractured legs.

Wounds and Punctures   If the puncture is caused by a foreign object (such as a nail in the foot), try to remove it gently

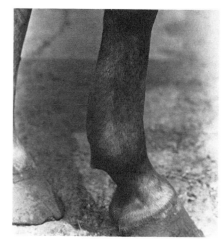

If your horse is suddenly very lame and you find heat, pain, and swelling in the area behind the cannon bone, your horse may have sprained a tendon.

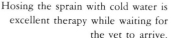

Hosing the sprain with cold water is excellent therapy while waiting for the vet to arrive.

yourself. If you can't, then wait until help arrives. If the wound is a tear, wash it and the surrounding area with warm water or use a hose. Don't apply any medication to the wound and don't give the animal any medication orally. If it is a gaping wound, apply a sterile bandage to the area to keep flies and dust from causing further contamination. Then call your vet. Depending on the wound, the vet may want to give your horse a tetanus booster and suture the laceration.

The horseman can easily treat small wounds. Carefully wash the wound and surrounding area, clipping back any hairs that protrude into the wound. Then apply some antibiotic ointment on a sterile gauze pad, place the pad over the wound, and bandage.

Miscellaneous and Sometimes Mysterious Symptoms   If you know your horse well and are an observant horseman, there may come a day when you look at your horse and *know* that something is wrong without being able to put your finger on the problem. Don't hesitate—call your vet. The chances are that your horseman's intuition is absolutely correct and something is wrong. In fact, there are a number of symptoms, some more obvious than others, the appearance of which should be relayed to your vet. For instance, if your horse suddenly stops eating, appears depressed, appears to be constipated or has diarrhea, has a cough or a runny nose, is running a temperature in excess of 103°F, is sweating and appears distressed or anxious, and behaves abnormally for any length of time, call your vet. Since your horse is totally dependent on you for all his care, but especially medical attention, it is far better to be safe than sorry.

GLOSSARY

Action   The way in which the horse moves his legs in the walk, trot, and canter.

Aids   Signals given to the horse that communicate the rider's instructions.

Appointments   Equipment and clothing used in showing and hunting.

Barren   A mare not in foal.

Bascule   The arc made by the horse's body when jumping.

Braids   When the mane is plaited, each plait is called a braid.

By   Sired by a particular stallion.

Cast   When a horse rolls close to a stall wall and, as a result, gets stuck, he is said to be cast. Also, a stiff bandage used to immobilize fractures or strains.

Colic   A gastric disturbance resulting in violent pain. Because colic can be fatal, it is a medical emergency.

Conformation   The shape or physique of a horse.

Counter-canter   A canter on the wrong lead intentionally. Also called a false canter.

Dam   The mother of a horse.

Disposition   The temperament of a horse.

Estrus   Heat or season, when the mare will accept a stallion.

Firing   An operation performed by veterinarians to cure some lameness caused by injuries to the tendons and ligaments.

Floating   The filing down of the horse's teeth with a rasp.

Flying change   A lead change executed at a canter or gallop with no interruption of pace.

Forehand   The head, shoulders, and front legs of the horse.

87

Forging When the horse hits his front foot with his hind foot.

Gelding A castrated (or altered) male horse.

Gestation The length of time between conception and birth. In a horse, it is eleven months.

Get A stallion's progeny.

Head shy A horse who jerks his head away when touched is said to be head shy.

Heaves A horse with heaves shows considerable breathing distress during exercise and tries to empty his lungs by "heaving" with his diaphragm. Similar to emphysema in humans.

Hunter A horse used as a show hunter or a field hunter.

Incisors Front teeth.

Interfere When a horse hits one leg with the opposite foot, he is said to interfere.

Jumper A horse used for his jumping ability in the show ring.

Light horse A horse used primarily for riding.

Longe To exercise a horse in a circle around the handler at the end of a thirty-foot longe line.

Mare An adult female horse.

Pace The horse's rate of speed.

Passage An elevated trot.

Premium list Also called an entry form. A sheet or booklet describing the classes of a horse show.

Proud flesh Rapidly growing tissue that sometimes forms on wounds, especially leg wounds.

Ringbone An arthritic, bony enlargement occurring either on the pastern or just above the coronary band.

Schooling Practicing exercises to improve the education and skills of both horse and rider.

Scouring Diarrhea in the horse.

Show A competition consisting of different categories and classes in which horse and rider are judged.

Sidebones The hardening of the lateral cartilage of the horse's foot.

Sire The father of a horse.

Sponsor Someone who takes over the care, feeding, and exercising of a horse for a fee. This arrangement is also called leasing.

Strangles The equine version of distemper, strangles is a highly contagious disease.

Transitions   The changes among the various gaits or paces.

Traverse   Side steps, without forward or backward movement.

Twitch   A vicelike device used to control the horse; usually applied to the upper lip.

Waxing   When milk starts to drip from the mare's udder, the process is called waxing.

Wind puffs   Small swellings usually around the fetlocks. Also called wind galls.

SUGGESTED FURTHER READING

Burn, Barbara. *The Horseless Rider.* New York: St. Martin's, 1979.

Harris, Susan. *Grooming to Win.* New York: Scribner, 1977.

Lose, M. Phyllis, D.V.M. *Blessed are the Brood Mares.* New York: Macmillan, 1978.

Naviaux, James L., D.V.M. *Horses in Health and Disease.* New York: Arco, 1967.

Richter, Judy. *Horse and Rider: From Basics to Show Competition.* New York: Simon & Schuster, 1979.

INDEX

91

ABOUT THE AUTHOR

"I was born in England in 1936 and was horse crazed from infancy (to the amazement of my parents, who were not). In spite of the war and a total lack of funds, I somehow wangled my way into Pony Clubbing, exercising other people's horses. I was able to exercise racehorses later on. I came to the United States in 1959 and eventually married a saintly man who has patiently put up with my horse mania over the years. We have three children (two stepchildren and one of our own) and we live on a 200-acre ranch right on the Pacific Ocean, twenty miles north of San Francisco. Several years ago I started my own boarding stable, and I now take care of about forty-five horses. I also teach children to ride, put on horse shows, write articles, and take care of my family. I became an American citizen in 1967."

LARAMIE JR. HIGH IMC

DATE DUE

JAN 7 2003			
	45-230		Printed in USA